Am I Crazy?

Am I Crazy?

POETRY

Ves'Shawna Jackson

Xulon Press

Xulon Press
2301 Lucien Way #415
Maitland, FL 32751
407.339.4217
www.xulonpress.com

© 2020 by Ves'Shawna Jackson

All rights reserved solely by the author. The author guarantees all contents are original and do not infringe upon the legal rights of any other person or work. No part of this book may be reproduced in any form without the permission of the author. The views expressed in this book are not necessarily those of the publisher.

Unless otherwise indicated, Scripture quotations taken from the Holy Bible, New International Version (NIV). Copyright © 1973, 1978, 1984, 2011 by Biblica, Inc.™. Used by permission. All rights reserved.

Scripture quotations taken from the English Standard Version (ESV). Copyright © 2001 by Crossway, a publishing ministry of Good News Publishers. Used by permission. All rights reserved.

Scripture quotations taken from the King James Version (KJV) – *public domain*.

Printed in the United States of America.

ISBN-13: 978-1-6312-9862-2

Dedication

I Thank God for YOU who are reading this book, and ask that God touch and bless you right now. Even as you read these words, an overwhelming peace will come upon you. In Jesus Name!

My Children

JaShai—My First Prize: Words cannot express how deeply my love runs for you. We grew up together, learned together, struggled together, you and I. No one can separate us. But God kept us.

Juakin—You are such a special, mature young man. Ever since you were an infant, I knew that there was something different about you, such a charmer and caretaker of your mom. I love you in a special way.

JreShawn—I'm chuckling as I write this. You're amazing! Just one look into those big droopy eyes will make any heart melt. You're intellectual and charming; smooth, protective, and kind-hearted. I love you to pieces, my chocolate. Yum!

Ms. Llondyn—My living proof that "all things work together for those who love the Lord." You brighten my life, my "mini" me. I always said I wanted a new and improved Shawna. God knew what He was doing, giving you to me in my latter years. You are so very special to me. Though I know you're only mine for a while, I will love, care for you, and protect you like the jewel you are, my very own Princess.

Shout-Out to my siblings—Veania, Shiniece, Niyoka, Elliotte, Tyshieme—I love you to pieces. I wish and pray nothing but the best for you.

My Father—You have always been an awesome Man and supportive father. You are one of a kind—I truly Love you.

I thank God for the Beal family for supporting me with our children.

Shout-out to all of those who spoke into my life and didn't hold back what God had to say to and about me. It is this which allowed me to continue to stand and not give up.

Donna Davis- Your thorough expertise.

In Loving Memory of *Claudette "Tye" Barfield* The Queen

        To God Be the Glory!

Introduction

It is my prayer that you read this with intent and personalization. Grab hold and embrace what you read throughout the pages of this book, which is, in totality, the reality of my life. What better way to intrigue and enlighten you than through transparency. I've never liked to sugar coat, nor have anyone sugar coat for me. In fact, it is one of my pet peeves. I believe skating around subjects too much will eventually lead to a fall. Additionally, a false reality of the matter is created, and any chance of growth is hindered. Not addressing things in our lives directly creates a false reality. It keeps us at a place of blockage and stagnancy. We are unable to move forward and look past our current circumstances. It's dangerous!

Wake up! I say, through the power and authority that has been placed inside of me through Jesus Christ. Stand! Lift your head up without exalting yourself; lengthen your spine and broaden your shoulders. Act, think, look, and dress like who you want to be. Your beginning is not your end, unless you choose this for yourself.

Reveal and do not be exposed. You are one of a kind; yet, "nothing is new under the sun." You have the God-given power to transform yourself and to transform a generation that follows thereafter. Stop being selfish! This is not about you and never was.

Your experiences, your current circumstances, though personal, are for someone else; though internal, are meant to be shared; though sacred, are meant to free; though burdensome, are meant to bring relief; though bringing infirmity upon you, are meant to bring healing, refreshment, enlightenment, restoration. Your pain, which I will call trash, is for someone to discover their treasure.

Why are you still sick? "For everything there is a season." Come, let's try to figure "us" out.

I pray for our deliverance to occur throughout these pages. Uh oh! She said "deliverance," though some may shy away from the term when speaking about being bound. Yet, when a baby is delivered, it's a beautiful thing. This fact alone demonstrates all of our need for deliverance on some level.

The surface can be safe. Everything is visual on this level. What you see is what you get. It's safe here: a place of protection where we are our own shield. Oh, but the deep place! It can be scary, like drowning under water. You don't know what's going to happen. You cannot see what's in front of you, because the deep can be a dark place. Your guard has weakened. It appears that you are no longer capable of protecting yourself—defenseless. You are fighting to stay on the surface where it's safe.

However, it's the very surface that keeps you like a dead flower. No water. Oh, and the deep---is where everything dies that is not you.

Though we can see at surface level, we are blind and without vision. As I mentioned earlier, "What you see is what you get." Do you only want what you can see—unable to tap into anything outside of your situation or circumstances?

Do not remain in your false and dangerous place you call reality. Do not remain blind in your safe place because you can see—still, without vision; or stay because you're in control of an out-of-control situation. And dare someone try to enter your arena; skate, skate, skate.

In the place of deep, you are blind but with vision. You are aware that your circumstances are not healthy. You've come to a reality that it is unsafe to remain at surface level. You realize that your circumstances are out of control, and that they are out of your control. You are ready to allow people in. There is hope here.

Welcome. Take a deep breath.

Table of Contents

Dedication   vii
Introduction   ix
Walking on Water   1
Gene-Race-tion-al   6
Out of Water "You Are Nothing"   12
Who Is She?   16
Wo-Man!   20
Rejection   25
I Need a Me in My Life   30
Spotted Blue Crow   35
Tried and True   41
My Flesh Speaks Volumes   46
Mirror Mirror on the Wall   51
Jenga   56
More of You, Less of Me   61
Stranger   65
Base   70
Criti-Size   75
First Prize   81
Rock   86
Spotted Blue Crow Part 2 (Am I Crazy?) Again I ask: 91
Two Red Chairs   96
"SHUT UP AND FILL UP"   102
My First Love   107
Bio   113

Walking on Water

See, even though I was drowning, I was never alone. I felt like I was. I had no idea that my life would take a turn for the worse, nor did I know that it had to. I had to go under. It was the worst feeling and experience of my life. Yet, it was the surface level that was taking me under. The events in my life that I could see were affecting me, pulling me down. I fought to stay on the surface, but I went under. Literally, I was drowning. However, I was being kept—for a purpose. I went under so that I could learn to look beyond myself. See, I was lost while I was under. Picture yourself drowning, kicking and fighting for your life. In that moment, I learned to stop fighting. Stop fighting the unknown and just float.

Walking on Water

I'm under water,
Trying to find my way to safety.

I'm being filled, but by pollutants that surround me.
I'm under water, but I'm thirsty.
I survived the tsunami; yet, still seeking refuge.

I'm drowning.

I'm fighting.

I used to be such a good swimmer.
My strength is dwindling.

I used to be such a good swimmer.

My arms are growing weak,
My legs unsteady.

How will I ever make it to shore?

Quick, think!
I can't.

The sound waves in my brain are still,
As the movement of the waters around me are steadfast in their movement.

Quick, call for help!

Picture what comes out when opening your mouth under water. Ugh.

I used to swim so well.
I look to my left, to my right, down. Lift your head up.

But I'm drowning. This may be the end.
Something's happened.
I can't swim like I used to.

My coordination is suffering.
As the water rises, I'm a desert. Deserted.

I used to swim so well. I'm tired.

I'm done.

My arms, legs…
Suddenly I'm floating.

Lying still but floating.
Sand.

Oh my God.

I survived the tsunami.

Yet, the "real" battle has just begun.

Walking on Water

Reflection:

Think about your present situation or a circumstance you have endured. You didn't think you would make it out. It's a dark place; to see a way out is ridiculous. You have little confidence that anything will change in this place; your actions/words are reflections of your thoughts. The things you do to come out of this place are temporary fixes, or should I say Band-Aids—defense mechanisms that only cover the hurt—and when exposed, all hell breaks loose.

Question:

What circumstances are you in or have gone through that you appeared to have come out of? Have you learned from them, grown from them? Do you have a new mindset, and are you now walking a path opposite the path opposite the path that almost took you under? Or are you continuing on the same path, while this time expecting the result to be different?

Walking on Water
(scripture)

Blessed are the poor in spirit, for theirs is the kingdom of heaven. Blessed are those who mourn, for they shall be comforted. Blessed are the meek, for they shall inherit the earth....

(Matthew 5: 3-5)

Gene-Race-tion-al

It's only when you acknowledge where you came from, that you will be able to see clearly, where you are going. From the time we were in the womb, others have contributed to depositing in us. We held no power, up to a point, to do anything other than receive. We were told: "Do as I say, not as I do." We had no control over the environment into which we were born. This environment has shaped us. Blood flows through generations. But we can choose to change the direction in which it flows.

Gene-Race-tion-al

Gene-
A Unit of heredity that is transferred from a parent to an offspring and held to determine some characteristic of the offspring.

Race-
A group of people united or classified together on the basis of common history, nationality, or geographic distribution.

tion-
Indicating state, condition, action, process, or result.

al-
Relating to; of the kind of.

I was born cursed.
The origin of my creation soon became innate. I am you and you are me.
What you have become will become a part of me.

According to genetics, I am you and you are me.

"Culturally" we are one.
Blended together, we are "family."
We are one.

The foundation, or lack thereof, that was set before me, becomes me.
The tools, or lack thereof, you were equipped with, will be used to equip me.
Or maybe not.
And so I lack.
Or I gain.

You were raised, or maybe you raised yourself. But now, who will raise me?
Who are you?
Do you know?
Who will raise me?

Who was Great Grandma?
Grandma was a product.
You are a product.
And now I'm here.

But who is raising me?

I'm beginning to see a pattern, As I look within our "culture."

As the scale of my life called age rises, my vision clears, wise-dominion (wisdom) is gained;
through time and experience, systems within the "culture" read like a quilt;
all different shades, beautiful. Beautiful colors and designs, vibrancy, shapes...
Lol, yeah that's us.

Hmmm, a quilt! A quilt is a cover. Beautifully made on the outside, It can be used as an ornament to hide what's beneath... This part isn't funny.

See, as I work to uncover what's beneath my beautifully patterned place on the quilt,
I smell an aroma of something that's been covered "beautifully" too long,
An aroma that was coming from me, but now I'm free.

So I pull away...

I remain a part of the quilt; yet, my pattern has changed.

I was born alone, an individual.

Gene-Race-tion-al

Reflection:

When you evaluate where you come from, we all have some good and some not so good (generational curses & blessings) passed down, which contribute to who we are. There are even things we believed were good or were good for a season, but are not favorable to our present season. There comes a time when you must set out to find your own identity, apart from whom you were molded by your environments and bloodlines to be—whether through parents, family, society, teachers, peers, boyfriends, girlfriends—and turn to the One who created you. Now that you have life, use every day to pursue your purpose.

Question:

What traditions are you holding on to, being faithful to, that are not being faithful to you, and that are not getting you any closer to your purpose?

Gene-Race-tion-al
(scripture)

I will establish my covenant as an everlasting covenant between me and you and your descendants after you for the generations to come, to be your God and the God of your descendants after you.

(Genesis 17:7)

Out of Water
"You Are Nothing"

My head was lifted. I had conquered many obstacles as a result of my own strength. The more I conquered, the more confident I became in my own abilities. I became wiser in my own eyes as I went through and came through. In more areas than one, I was becoming more and more built up. What I did do, I did well; what I knew, made sense. Everything was put together in a nice little package. Still, so much was missing that I was not aware of.

Out of the Water
"You Are Nothing"

Arise, you are nothing.

You will be, but you never were.

All that you are, you're nothing.

Your clothes are fine and well put together like a masterpiece; like creativity lives in your bones, runs through veins, travels through your blood, and seeps through your flesh.

You Are Nothing. Your mind is sharp.
Your wisdom flows like it's from the soul of an elderly woman whose mother was wise.
But you're nothing.

You're hated by few, loved by many. Your company is plenty, and you're welcomed by any.

They love to be among you You're Nothing.

The sex opposite to you is attracted, intrigued by what you have to offer.

But you have nothing. Well, who are you?

The writer? She's a nobody,

Telling you that you are somebody, once you become nothing.

Out of the Water
"You Are Nothing"

Reflection:

When you think about your present position in life, you may be in a good place: successful, happy, able to provide for your children, healthy. You may be in a place where you do not have the fullness of these things, but you are content. You have people in your life who love you; you get the attention you feel that you deserve. But, what's left if any of these things ever go lacking?

Question:

In all you are and all you do, who's benefitting? Have you returned anything to the One who gave you your existence, or are you just enjoying your existence? Or, do you really have the mindset that you are nothing and need to be reassured that, through your Creator, you are "beautifully and wonderfully made"? Have you yet come to a place where you recognize your human weaknesses? Have you acknowledged them? Have you surrendered them?

You Are Nothing
(scripture)

But by the grace of God I am what I am: and His grace which was bestowed upon me was not in vain...

(1 Corinthians 15:10)

Who Is She?

"Love me or hate me?" is the question. People tend to surf the outer appearance of another being. With distinct observation, they come to a conclusion about what they think they see. Thoughts and perspectives form in their minds, only to determine how they will treat that individual. I learned that to know a person, you have to know them. Seeing them is just a carnal view of a spiritual being.

Who Is She?

Her presence is captivating as she maneuvers about.
The room she enters becomes still; the atmosphere shifts.
Among parties, communication becomes distinct as their focus shifts.
Thoughts emerge; conversations continue, though boggled.

Down to her style and the way she wears her clothes, she's creative.
Caressing every curve, her attire fits like a glove.
Her hair, never out of place and suiting to her outfit, Complimenting her attire down to her shoe type.

Gracefully, classily, forceful, dominant, piercing and with poise... Her stride is of confidence, strength and pride, and expression of gravity and significance.
The wind captures and spreads a mist, the admiration and inspiration left behind.
Envy develops in shallow hearts and weak minds.

From the core flows her conversation. Her eyes search the souls of another.
From the core, passion and wantonness flow; yet, integrity and justness.
Heartfelt, explicit, eager and humble; yet, superficial, mysterious and apathetic and prideful.
Relatable, accommodating and easygoing; yet, adverse, selfish, and intolerant.

Her body language translates sexiness; in agreement her posture is a countenance.
Astonishingly beautiful, yet flawed. Flaws and all, she stands tall; all in all...
Spreading what she has... what does she have? Who is she?

Who are you?

Who am I?

Who Is She?

Reflection:

We can sometimes wear masks or wear clothes… to cover our inner turmoil. We cannot heal our souls overnight, but we can hide behind a nice outfit, hairdo, makeup, and a fake smile; all the while, fooling those who are easily fooled by mere outer appearance. You're alive and vibrant on the outside, but lifeless and numb on the inside.

Question:

What are you covering up, and what is your cover-up (clothes, cars, drugs, alcohol, sex…)? Is your confidence screaming insecurity?

Who Is She?
(scripture)

Jesus said, "For judgement I came into this world, that those who do not see may see, and those who see may become blind.

(John 9:39)

Wo-Man!

I am not married, nor have I ever been. I gave birth to my first child when I was 17 years old. At that tender age, I had the mindset that if my child's father did not want to help, then I would do it by myself. I'm not going to force any man to take care of my child, to do his job as a father. Watch me do this. A woman can raise a man to be a man. A father figure is not needed. Boy, was I young-minded—and wrong.

Wo-Man!

No, I am a woman.
Out of my Wo-mb came a child.

Grace be to God; He allowed us to become one to produce another human being.

How mean.

There was no covenant between…Covenant, we knew nothing of. Yet, a union allowed by God.

Why—did God allow this union?

I guess I could have stayed while continuing to get played, but I had to go,
Or else lose the very strength that I would need to take care of your seed, because God knew you weren't going to—play your position.

Did He know that I would try to? So I'm left to—play your position.

Two hats I'm wearing; yet, one of them doesn't seem to fit. And the shoes? Way too big.
Yet, I'm wearing both.

With these oversized fits, a hidden figure I must be, which, when it wasn't hidden, you had no problem being there. And now, the one figure is hidden, and apparently you didn't pass math, because that equals—I need help.

continued

Wearing an oversized hat, yet uncovered.
Shoes too big, thus room for error. And my child... Exposed,
Susceptible to another disaster.
But I got this.

See, my role I know, and yours, I'm adapting to.

Hmmm, I wonder why I'm off, angry, bitter, frustrated...
weighed down.
My compassion, love, sensitivity...were becoming numb.

Unconsciously, I attempted to play your position, fill your shoes, to give what you didn't, to go where you wouldn't, love like you couldn't, to be present like you weren't, and to chastise like you--- weren't in position to do.

Wo-Man!

I'm a Woman.

Wo-Man!

Reflection:

I believe that giving birth to anything (child, gift...) should not be taken lightly. It takes more than one person to take care of something while in the womb, and once birth is given. Every decision you make prior to conception will reflect the aftermath. Unfortunately, the math doesn't always add up.

Question:

Are you dealing with the aftermath of a premature mindset?

Wo-Man!
(scripture)

Then the Lord God said, "It is not good that the man should be alone; I will make him a helper fit for him."

(Genesis 2:18)

Rejection

I learned late in life that I was a product of rejection. The things you learn about yourself when allowing personal growth to take place in your life! I did not expect to be rejected, which is why it's such a harsh reality. When I searched, I did not find. So easily shunned. Why? I don't know. However, I now realize that sometimes you have to be rejected to find who you are, whose you are, and where you belong.

Rejection

Don't turn away. She'll get offended.

Don't say the wrong thing. She'll get defensive.

Don't tell her, you don't like what she has on, that what she's doing is wrong, ask why she took so long, why this poem isn't a song.

Don't test her. She's demanding.

Maybe.

She's tired.

True.

She's fearful.

Fearful of facing another's back, Several steps she takes back

As they walk away.

She's mad. She's hurt.

She's optimistic,

Enough to give another try to the very spy that she dare not let see her cry.

Why?

If there was a dry Kleenex in the room, dry it would remain. To wipe the tears from her eyes would be to waste a dry substance of perfection.

Spy?

She finds that your presence in her life denotes a love that's "undercover,"
Mimics the title; yet, the information you deliver is futile, sabotaging...

There goes your back again. I ought to stab...

That's not who she is. She stands alone.
Is this her purpose?

The choice is not her own.
The love that was shown was limited.
Now for her to give you her back is innate.

Rejection

Reflection:

Consider your life.
Consider your mindset, actions, and choices to be roots (strong beliefs developed through life events on which you depend.)

I'll give you a bonus here:
Personal example: My facing so much rejection resulted in a mindset of wanting to be accepted. My mindset changed from a once independent mindset to: let me try to fit in and make people like "accept" me. And so the choice I made resulted in me acting in ways, talking in ways, and doing things in ways that I may not have done otherwise if the seed of rejection hadn't been planted in me.

Question:

What are some mindsets that you have developed because of experiences (seeds planted), which resulted in certain actions you portray and choices you've made? Are you living a lifestyle that is not you as a result of negative seeds that have turned into belief systems you hold?

Rejection
(scripture)

As you come to Him, a living stone rejected by men but in the sight of God chosen and precious.

(1 Peter 2:4)

I Need a Me in My Life

Apparently, I'm a giver. I give my time. I give my advice. I give my ear. I give my money. I give my love, my loyalty, my consistency, my strength, my weakness, my understanding and encouragement. I give my word. No, I am not perfect, but I aim to be that person in someone's life that I would want them to be in mine. I learned that when you are a giver, people fail to realize that you yourself have needs. My stature is that of a nurturer. Yet, the very ones I yearned to develop seemed to have no problem with receiving my provision. I guess I should have never expected a return. My nature should have won many over, one would think. Nevertheless, I have struck out with many. I always wondered why this was my story.

I Need a Me in My Life

Though I am blessed, I feel alone. Though I am chosen, I feel alone.
Though I know that my latter days will be more bountiful than my present,
I feel alone.

I trust wholeheartedly in God; He is consistent, never wavering...
Yet, I feel as if everyone I can see is a complete opposite.

I know... "Trust no man..." But geesh, I feel alone.

Who, to a humanly extent can I reach out to and rely on? I feel alone.

With so much to offer and so much to give and willing, But when it comes to me...
Who, on earth, can I lean on and confide in, When I need a dime or two?

Who will understand the depth in which my soul runs?
Who will not run and spread the good news of my weakness? The fact that I, yes I, need someone.

Who is capable of looking beyond the surface?
Who is not surreal in their thoughts, and thus actions?
Who has the common knowledge not to judge my book by its cover?

Are you reading these words? Or have you already judged my book by the cover?
I encourage you to keep reading.

continued

Who has the mental strength not to judge me according to what they think they see,
Or what they have allowed their minds to be influenced to think?

People kill me, Weak minded.

Reasons for resentment towards me are created.

The spirit of insecurity leaves one unable to celebrate what they cannot fathom in me.
Don't compare yourself to who you perceive me to be.
Your dislike towards me is according to your scale that does not measure up.
Fix the scale!

It's broken. And so you are.

But who said I didn't... Have insecurities? Ok.
Don't openly love my reality while secretly hating the person.

Your opinion has been formed.
There you stand with you false reality of me. When you're done, encourage me.

A trying time—to whom do I turn?
I am misunderstood and my passion is shunned. I need a me in my life.

I Need a Me in My Life

Reflection:

It's good to have at least one person in your life to share your wholehearted self with, someone you feel so comfortable with. It's like you're having a conversation with yourself and no one is in the room; to have someone who understands you and even understands your lack of expression, that person who does not compete with you, and only wants the best for you. You know, like you.

Question:

Where do you turn when you want to be you?
When you reach a point where you no longer care what others think, and are no longer trying to be accepted. Do you love you enough to release this behavior and allow God to step in and bring those into your life who are meant to be there?

I Need a Me in My Life (scripture)

He gives strength to the weary and increases the power of the weak.

(Isaiah 40:29)

Spotted Blue Crow

I could tell that something in me was changing. I had no idea what; nor did I have any control over what was transpiring. Oh, I tried to control what was becoming out of control. The more I tried to control it, the more out of control it became. I developed the best plan I could come up with. Nevertheless, I had already lost my grip. I held on as tightly as I could, for as long as I could. This strange feeling I felt, I had never felt before. It was new to me. I could not put a name to what was going on.

Spotted Blue Crow

Where did you come from? Were you hiding out?
Waiting for the appropriate moment to make your appearance?
How rude! You didn't take the time to introduce yourself.
Though, I wish I'd never met you.

The sudden rush made me blush. Oh the sudden rush
made me blush.
The things you put my body through, And so suddenly,
Taking me through all these changes.

The sudden rush of your touch makes my heart beat. Oh, how my
heart beats.
My head pounds at the very thought of your presence.
My stomach?

When you are with me,
you are first, and the very fact that my body needs nourishment
becomes a distant need.
My weight diminishes.
The intensity of your presence overtakes me down to my very
appearance.

What are you doing to me?
I've never experienced such a force.
I've always had control.

My mind is like a worm.
I can't seem to keep it off of you.
My death will come soon, right after my mind is "blown."
You're like a fluid,
running through my veins in the place of my blood,
Paralyzing me to the point of speech-less.

And so I write.

I am social, no longer. Your force is magnetizing.
As your magnitude increases, my solitude decreases.
What are you doing to me?
I know it's not just me.
Everyone notices the change in me,
Since you have attached yourself to me.
Oh, God! They notice the change in me.

I have never had a relationship of such that puts me through so much,
Where not an inch of me is untouched.
How much longer will you be here, and will I allow your attachment?

I want to separate myself from you.
You got me.
You have me on lockdown.
The force behind your clinginess conflicts like a tug of war.
No one has ever had me like this.
I usually have control.

Should I take flight?
Or stay and fight for what's mine?
My shine is no more.
You dimmed the light I once had.
Now I'm just a shadow.

Trying to be heard,
But I'm speech-less.

And so I write.

continued

I said I would never be in an abusive relationship.

I usually am in control.
But no more.
I am control-less.

Thank you.

Anxiety.

Spotted Blue Crow

Reflection:

Consider your present circumstance. You may, or may not, be up against some trials and struggles. You continue on, because, though there are occurrences, you have managed to duck and dodge and not be taken under by them. You may even be continuing in a situation or mindset that screams danger, but it's familiar; so you remain.

Question:

Are you mentally, physically, emotionally, and spiritually in position for a suddenly moment?

Spotted Blue Crow
(scripture)

When anxiety was great within me, your consolation brought me joy.

(Psalms 94:19)

Tried and True

We all go through a period in our lives where we are learning who we are, trying to get in where we fit in. I, myself, have never hung in groups; neither did I ever find a group in which I wanted to be included, outside of my family. We all know—family is where it all begins. I was being molded, or should I say, I was the potter? I changed sizes, attitudes, demeanors… many times, according to who I thought I needed to be, or who people expected me to be. When molding, the substance is to become a sizable and beautiful masterpiece. However, I had shrunk and developed a presence that was unattractive.

Tried and True

I cannot seem to find where this piece belongs. It's been a while... I think I've tried every angle, viewed every aspect, acknowledged every precept.

This piece still does not fit.

Initially, this piece was perfect. A perfect fit shall I say.
This piece was distorted, Yeah, maybe.

And so I attempted to force this piece to fit. Like a plague, this piece was unwelcome.
The mold of this piece was not suited to the big picture.
Something is wrong with this piece.

More adjustment is needed. I know this piece belongs.
I'm strong.
So I will not quit.

I think I got it!
The portrayal of this piece calls for a definite fit.
Bit by bit, this piece is becoming a part of the big picture.
Yet, this piece is stubborn.

Though outwardly it's sizing up to fit nicely, There's a preconception on displacement. Amazingly, I have not given up.

I'm tough.
So I will not quit.

It's not that complicated. Mind over matter;
I can work this thing.

This piece is last,
hence, stands out from the big picture. In this case, my view is like crystal.

As I continue to mold this piece, smaller it becomes, and more distorted. Bigger becomes the picture,
and clearer my view. See, this piece is she.
She was never meant to be "A part of."

She was last, so that she might come first.

She did not fit so that she would become lost. Once she became lost, she was found.
Once she was found, she came to know Who she was,

And to whom, she belongs.

Tried and True

Reflection:

You have reached your destination, or not so much. You have reached a halt in your life, where you are unable to adjust, twist, wiggle, fake… uh oh! Now you have to face… YOU.

Question:

Are you ready to face you, or will you continue to make face? Are you willing to be set apart in order to become a part of the puzzle? Are you ready to be reshaped, made, and molded into a masterpiece, or will you remain just a piece?

Tried and True
(scripture)

You are the light of the world. A town built on a hill cannot be hidden.

(Matthew 5:14)

My Flesh Speaks Volumes

Sex appeal is so important in today's society. There was a time where this was also priority for me. My relationships would be prioritized according to appearance, then what the person could contribute. Well, my criteria were based on a foundation that would take me through more agony than I cared to experience. And so now, I walk away from your presence for a different reason.

My Flesh Speaks Volumes

My mind is constantly in thought.
I'm thinking of ways to better myself,
to elevate.

I have goals, and I will stop at nothing until they're accomplished.
I'm thinking: What can I do that can in turn be used to
benefit others?

Hmmm, improving my life can later improve the life of another. I
have a teaching spirit.
I have a good heart, though it's been broken.

I try to live in an attempt to be an inspiration, leave a legacy. I
have standards and a spirit of integrity.

Not only do I want to succeed,
I want to witness the success of others.

I'm concerned and interested in the history and present of
my culture.

My mind is constantly in thought regarding the when's of why.

I like intense conversations that produce thoughts and turn
into action.

I like searching the minds of others and don't mind if *minds* is
searched in the process.

My patience is short with the lack of others,
though, I'm aware that I have my own areas of needed
improvement.

continued

I have been through some trials that have affected my present existence.

As I grow, I learn more and more of these afflictions.

I have found and developed a relationship with God that has begun this journey.

Little by little, step by step… I am evolving more and more. God has given me a new set of "eyes."
The when's of why are becoming clearer; my heart is being mended and my spirit refreshed…

My afflictions, I can now acknowledge and address.

I'm on this journey…
It's not an easy one…

I may have something to offer you as my tests evolve into a testimony.

Wanna hear?
Wanna have one of those intense conversations that I'm so intrigued by?

Hello?…

I'm sorry.

I'm boring you.

But I can see that you're enticed by the language that my hips, thighs, and backward view is speaking.

Well, watch them, as I walk away.

My Flesh Speaks Volumes

Reflection:

Consider your thought process. Consider the dreams that you have for yourself, which others may or may not be aware of—those times you are alone, when your mind begins to wander and lands in a place consisting of fulfilled dreams, and you.

Question:

How often have you laid these dreams to the side for someone who only wants to lay you down, and has no dreams of their own? How often have you given yourself, along with your dreams/passions, all for nothing to be gained? When will you realize that it's not they, but you, who are killing your own dreams?

My Flesh Speaks Volumes
(scripture)

Charm is deceitful, and beauty is in vain, but a woman who fears the Lord is to be praised.

(Proverbs 31:30)

Mirror Mirror on the Wall

Dear Mom,

You probably did not know how much I loved you.

See, I was distant, and the distance was a manifestation of my broken heart. I knew you loved me. But I was young and lacked the wisdom to understand that you just loved me differently. See, I went by my feelings and what my eyes could see. And I clearly was not your favorite. Well, as my vision became clearer, I knew that the love that was given to me was given from the shoes in which you walked. And now I understand that we all wear different sizes.

Though we wore different sizes, I respect the path you walked in your shoes.

Mirror Mirror on the Wall

Before you judge me, try my shoes. Take the time
To see why in my mind… There's a thin line between Our togetherness
And me resenting you.

My nerves you weigh on
Like a burden I can't shake.
Take, take, take.
That's you.
But I can't take you,

Though I love you
And see through to who you are
And who "we" can be.
But you…

You are seemingly like fine wine.
Ageing,
yet getting better with time,
While my mind is suffering.

Why do you pretend not to be in bondage?

See, once upon a time
I had a juvenile mind.
I perceived like a child,
understood like a child,
and received like a child

A woman I am;
In bondage I stand.
See, I stand.

Slowly unveiling myself,
Layers…
Geesh, this is thick,
But I stand
Because I chose to stand.
Regardless of not knowing who I am,
I face persecution,
And from you.

See, a lack of understanding both sides reflect.

Unconsciously, I had to walk in your shoes.
You continued to wear them.
More than slightly worn, you handed them off to me.

At the time, I couldn't see.
But transferrable the spirits were to me,
And now, "Am I Crazy?"

Though the reflection in your mirror may be flawed,
I take full responsibility for the woman I have become.

I stand flaws and all.

I too have shoes to pass down.

Mirror Mirror on the Wall

Reflection:

Consider someone in your life who is or was close to your heart, and who you felt hurt you. You don't understand why this person's love towards you was flawed. You spend years of your life just trying to understand.

Question:

Are you holding on to un-forgiveness, hurt, resentment, pride in your heart, yet love towards someone? Have you taken the time to put yourself in their shoes, and understand them? Release them and yourself and allow genuine love to come in?

Mirror Mirror on the Wall (scripture)

Behold, I was brought forth in iniquity, and in sin did my mother conceive me.

(Psalms 51:5)

Jenga

I couldn't understand why this would be my story. I sure was not everyone's cup of tea. I had no problem with making friends, but as soon as another player came on board, they were gone—as if I never existed. When I played, I played hard. Loyalty for me is important. For others, it was but a game. They played as long as there was a benefit. But as soon as they felt as if they were losing—off to another team.

Jenga

"For where there are two or three gathered..." (Matthew 18:20).
Seeking my other player.
I don't have time for games; yet, have been chosen to play this one, and it takes two.

But I'm tired.

I've found several players; getting them to stay until the end is like a game within itself.

Back at it again.

Still in my position.
Risking my life, because I have a vision.
I'm going to win.
Yet, it takes two.
I'm still seeking.

If I don't win, we all lose—the pressure.

If I don't stand, we all stumble—overwhelming.

If I don't rise, we all fall—the burden.

If I give up, I miss my destiny—the risk.

But my rise has become my doom.

Isn't the object of the game to come out on top, when it's all said and done, to stand?

Well, I'm standing.
But am I on top?

continued

I don't want to play; yet, I've been chosen.

Well, where are my players?

At least one will do the trick. I'm waiting.

Still in position.

As my players withdraw, the structure becomes taller and seemingly stronger, more equipped to balance it all; but, truly becoming more weakened and less structured.

Ok, focus!

Oh yeah, back at it again.

Focus.

Stand.

The players will come.

Jenga

Reflection:

Consider yourself lucky to have experienced genuine give and take relationships. Consider yourself blessed for these relationships to be genuine and long lasting.

Question:

Do you know that the Bible says: "The strong should carry the infirmities of the weak?" Have you any players on your team who will help you win? Or are they players who only stick around when the game is in their favor?

Jenga
(scripture)

They went out from us, but they were not of us; for if they had been of us, they would have continued with us. But they went out, that it might become plain that they all are not of us.

(1 John: 2:19)

More of You, Less of Me

I had reached a point where I was too much. Yes, I was so much, but was empty inside. I was beginning to learn what I had inside of me and who placed it. I began to yearn for it to manifest. My flesh weakened; still, I grew in my desire for spiritual growth. There is so much more to me and in me, and I wanted to walk in it. I wanted to experience something more than myself. However, I would have to die.

More of You, Less of Me

More of you, Less of Me,
Yet, you say I am complete in thee.
So why do I hunger?
For what I seek is already inside of me.
For I am full in thee.
My asking for more, is that gluttony?
I'm starved; I'm thirsty,
But you say that my belly is already that of a pregnant woman.
So I'm bloated?
No, you're complete.
So I'm whole?
Not within yourself, but within Me.
So I'm full?
Not of Me, but of yourself.
So you must be emptied to be filled.
You are Not. But I AM.

More of You, Less of Me

Reflection:

Consider yourself a masterpiece. You were created by Thee Master, and in Him you are lacking nothing. And there is no one like you! Apart from the Master, you are a mere piece. In math, this is a portion of a whole.

Question:

Are you complete? Are you full of yourself, or are you whole? Are you willing to become empty and be filled?

More of You, Less of Me (scripture)

She does not ponder the path of life; her ways wander, and she does not know it

(Proverbs 5:6)

Stranger

I felt so strange in a familiar place, a place I've been all of my life. I was fine, until my mind took me to a place to which I am no longer accustomed. I found myself lost in this familiar place, seeking where I could fit; or with whom I can fit in, who will accept me. I found courage in liquid. But this was not it. I love my family. However, with family is not where you're always included—family ties as in closely woven together. I've learned that, sometimes, even families are a clique, and everyone just won't qualify.

Stranger
(A questionable season)

The times we had are unforgettable,
Always laughter and good times,
Several of us in a room.
Boy, oh boy, the personalities would bloom.

Strange, but the togetherness was meant
Maybe not to my own advantage.
I had a hint then...

I think I need a drink, or two, or...

I'm going with the flow of the togetherness
But I can't flow without
Something flowing through me.

How do I adjust in such a setting?

Wait. Who are you all?
Who am I?
You all look so familiar.

In sync, you all speak.
My words fall upon deaf ears.
Our togetherness is hindered.
Then quickly the conversation picks up and moves forward.

Ha ha ha.
Yeah, that was funny. Dare I engage?

Nothing is flowing through me.
I'm not a part of the togetherness.
Just me and my sobriety

This is not fun anymore. Good times?

Was I ever a part of the togetherness?

That question no longer remains.

Stranger

Reflection:

Consider the saying: "Fly on the wall."

Question:

Have you ever been present, but felt excluded? There, but not a part of? What are you doing to fit in?

Stranger (scripture)

I did not sit in the company of revelers, nor did I rejoice; I sat alone, because your hand was upon me, for you had filled me with indignation.

(Jeremiah 15:17)

Base

I am a lot of things. Some of which are innate; some of which are learned behaviors; some of which are protective barriers that I, myself, created; some of which reflect internal brokenness; some of which reflect my life as a whole. So you'd better think twice before you approach, as this pillar was not yet positioned.

Base

How dare you?

Yes, I am a Queen in my own right.
But, how dare you,
Place her on a pedestal?

You don't get to take what you see:
the fleshly, outer part of me.
Judge her accordingly,
and say that you'll choose me?

How dare you?
Her issues are hidden.
Or are you just blind?
The mask that she hides behind
Makes her hard to find.

Her outer shell is solid and stable;
Her interior is soft like a pillow,
And when pressed, explodes like a volcano.
As she keeps it together, sturdier her exterior becomes.
Her emotions become shallower.
She keeps it together.

Her heart is just as hard as her external covering...
But there's a covering over your eyes called selfish ambition.

How dare you
Come into her life when yours if full of strife,
Attempting to find refuge in what you think you see?
Yes, I am a Queen in my own right.
But how dare you place her on a pedestal?

continued

She fooled you huh?
No, you fooled yourself.
Judging her by her outer, fleshly particle.

How dare you?

Selfishly, you chose to become congruent with another
human being.
In an attempt to become whole with an opposite "half" of person,
you expected her tough exterior to act as a foundation…
How dare you?

Now you blame me
for what you could not see.
And now you're disappointed?
How dare you?

You learned, after all,
that her appearance does have flaws,
and her exterior will not act as a base for you to stand tall.
I'm trying to tell y'all.

I am nobody's Base.

Base

Reflection:

Consider the hand you were dealt. Oh well, you say, I guess I'll play the hell out of it. You're not realizing that because you appeared to have a good hand, you're a target for some who are looking to partner with you, as you appear to look like you're going to come out on top. Your hand is attractive to the ones who feel as if they've received a hand that to them wasn't even worth staying in the game for. So they sought the "winning team."

Question:

Are you really winning? Or are you just skilled at playing the hand you've been dealt, thus attracting the wrong teammates?

Base (scripture)

"We then that are strong ought to bare the infirmities of the weak, and not to please ourselves."

(Romans 15:1)

Criti-Size

I've heard it all. But nothing that was said even came close to who I really was. Not that I knew who I was. But I knew who I was not! I didn't understood why a person would attempt to sabotage another's character. I had a clue. It wasn't me that they were trying to sabotage, but who they envisioned me to be, or not to be. The blanks were filled with criticism. See, people criticize what they don't understand.

Criti-Size

Look at her
as she walks,
as she talks,
as she moves about life.

Like a carefree woman,
not bothered by this life,
Like a pilgrim she walks,
untouched or unmoved by people.

Their actions?

Whatever.
Like a pilgrim she will walk.

And she walked.

And she walked some more.

Wow, the hate is real!
Yet, she's not doing anything real.
Or is she?
Is this she?
Is this who she is?

Ouch!
The sting of a jealous "outsider."
Shake it off.
Keep moving.

More shots fired!

Her head held high and keeps rising higher.

Ouch!

Another shot taken.

The holes in her may be piercing,
but the pride in her, I mean "determination" within, will not permit her to fall.
Her head rises;
her life, she continues to live,

As if in a war and she the only enemy.
Her pride, I mean "determination" grew.

Whoa!
The fight in her.

Higher and higher her head rose.

Uh oh!

Her nose is in the air...

Boom, boom, boom!

She's dodging, as her pilgrimage image begins to tarnish.
Do you see her though?
Her look, her walk, her talk, and the way she moves about life remain;
though piercings in her become more and more elusive and her identity more shallow,
she will remain "determined," unmoved, untouched by the flames from the shots fired.

She dzoes have feelings;
her emotions move her;
she can feel the bruises from the holes within.

Still, like a pilgrim she walks.

continued

Her head held high; yet, faint her demeanor grows, reflections of bitterness in her attitude.
Wait. Attitude? Yes. She has a bad attitude.

How many more times must her ear hear and mind be held hostage by these words?

She walks.

Sista, do you need a ride?
No.

Her journey of determination continues.

The halt in her step from accepting your charity will hinder her pilgrim journey.

Sista, I can help you.
No.

Thank you.
I got this.

The determination in her reflects "strength," yet, her strength reflects pride; her pride reflects coldness.

Wait a minute. "Pride?"

Criti-Size

Reflection:

Consider the rapper Fifty Cents. He was said to be shot "nine times."

Question:

How many times were you shot down, but rose back up? Who measured you with their flawed measuring tool, and are you still living according to these false measurements?

Criti-Size
(scripture)

Who are you to pass judgement on the servant of another? It is before his own master that he stands or falls. And he will be upheld, for the Lord is able to make him stand.

(Romans 14:4)

First Prize

I was young. I did not, and could not, fathom the agony that would follow having a child out of wedlock, out of wisdom. I had this thing lock and key; yeah, out of wed-lock. If the other half chose not to step up, I'd step up in his place. I learned that a mother raising a child on her own—it can be done, but it is not ideal. The arrangement turned out not to be healthy for my child or me. The order arranged by God would lessen the likeliness of wounds that my first-born would endure. As the man is the covering, without him being in position as a husband leaves the mother/child uncovered, susceptible to anything. But God!

First Prize

I won first prize but lost the game.

I made a few mistakes along the way, but I endured to the end.

I won!

My figure 8 returned… Ok, that's beside the point.

I was and still am in love with you.

"You are my Everything."
Remember…? I used to sing that song to you.

I doubt it.

You always came first,
Even over the one who contributed to your formation.

All my decisions surround you.

My life accommodates your very existence.

Our relationship is now nonexistent.
A winner I remain.

See, we grew up together.

A woman, raising a boy to be a man.

Wait. She was no woman.

Wait…

That woman was a girl.

I didn't know.

But what I did know is that I've never won anything before.

You were my first trophy.

I had to keep, cover, and protect you,

Establish a space for you;
Free of debris and toxicity.
Keep you polished.

Pure from "gene-race-tion-al curses."

You needed air.
I let you breathe.

But I never intended for you to inhale the wrong things.

I still have a trophy.
This time the space I leave, I leave for God to come in,

My first-born,

My First Prize.

First Prize

Reflection:

Consider someone or something that is like your prized possession. Your love and protection for this thing is deep and crosses boundaries… because this thing is not yours to keep.

Question:

What in your life do you consider your prized possession? Do you know that everything in this life is temporary? See, what you possess is what you control. Do you know that you're not in control?

First Prize
(scripture)

Behold, Children are a heritage from the Lord, the fruit of the womb, a reward.

(Psalms 127:3)

Rock

You couldn't tell me that I was not doing the right thing, living the right way, and making the right decisions. I had developed a serious guard that, in actuality, was a barricade—a hindrance to my life.

Don't get me wrong, my guard did protect me, but in a way like a Band-Aid over a wound; bruised underneath, but covered with a protective barrier. If uncovered, I would be exposed, vulnerable, susceptible to . . . more disappointment. So I kept my shield.

Though I was protected, to an extent, I was numb—numb to truth, reality, love, trust, forgiveness, relationships . . . Picture bouncing anything off a rock (imagine). Better yet, try it; try carrying a nice size rock along with you on a daily basis. Or are you?

Rock

I'm hard.
Nothing or no one can get to or through—to me.

Like a rock, I'm solid.
Don't test me, or like a match to a matchbook—or a rock to another— I'm explosive.
Like granite, I'm decorative, multi-purposeful, talented.
I can build and I can tear down; oh yeah, I can tear down.

What? I'm a "rock." What do you expect?
However, when I speak of these things about my surface/exterior,
I am to speak truth in that the rock I speak of is not externally me,
but within me, and is my heart.

I speak of both, because the one cannot exist without the other.
For, "from my heart flow the issues of my life."

So I carry my rock.

Everywhere I go, it goes. It's heavy.
It weighs me down, nonetheless protects me.

See, I never had someone to protect me;
So I carry my rock with me just in case I have to "bust" somebody down.

See, it protects me.

And you, you can "rock" with me,
but you'll be rocking with me and my rock.

continued

Yet, the weight is too heavy to bear;
So I can't wait for you to go.
Then it'll be just me and my rock,
And to that weight, I'm accustomed.
And with you, my load becomes heavier.
Now roll.

See, one my rock and I have become; Yeah, we're "solid."

No one can "break" us up.

See, my rock is my core, And out of it springs . . .
See, the spring didn't flow until the rock was busted open. So I guess from my rock, you get nothing.

But see, stingy I'm not.
I've lent my rock to others.
My rock provided them support, protection, strength.

They didn't care for my rock like I do,
So I took it back.

Even tighter I held it.

See, my heart I exercised; Its muscle I built.
Its tone—weak.

In totality, she's solid, However, easily broken.

Rock

Reflection:

Consider pride: Something you cling to, you're proud of, protective and territorial over. You keep it sacred. But when you share it, it's with conditions. Consider that thing, and how if it's taken from you, you have nothing.

Questions:

What are you holding onto that's not meant for you to keep? What is it you cherish so much, you fear giving it to others, and thus it tarnishes your character?

Rock (scripture)

This day I call the heavens and the earth as witnesses against you that I have set before you life and death, blessings and curses. Now choose life, so that you and your children my live.

(Deuteronomy 30:19)

Spotted Blue Crow Part 2 (Am I Crazy?) Again I ask:

I continue to carry the burden of "anxiety," while carrying the infliction you placed on me. See, I'm growing stronger, yet becoming more broken. Huh? Yes. As the anxiety broke me down, I was left to build myself up. As I'm fighting, struggling to overcome this battle, I have to pretend that I'm not hurt by you criticizing my portrayal of normal, all while not feeling normal.

Spotted Blue Crow Part 2 (Am I Crazy?)

Does the intensity of your force intensify my senses?
My mind is confused.
My heart is pounding, along with my forehead.
Fearful? Yes.

My speech lies dormant and communication function is dysfunctional.
My mind is not aligned with the words that roll off of my tongue.
One is brilliant, while the other is fiercely flawed.

The connection is flawed.

I shy away from alliances.

Though encaged in this cocoon, my eyes still see.
My heart still beats.
I am still human.
Behind this smile are emotions.

This figure 8, there's a broken spirit and tarnished soul that lies beneath.

Oh, I have eyes that see, and a salty liquid comes out of them, too.

You run away, sometimes literally, at the very idea of the tone that comes from my lips, reaching your ears.

I see you. Remember, my eyes still see.
Oh, and my heart still beats,
Sometimes to the extreme.
I can't control it.
You can't tell,
Too focused on your self-interest.
And my words and the tone behind them... obviously deliver no penetration.
Deaf ears they fall upon.

Back into my cocoon I go,
Pinned down with emotions and strong opinions.

Offended by my awkwardness?
I apologize. I'll make my life and yours easier by staying away.
But now you're offended by my distance and attempt to be silent?

My own thoughts, I'll explore,
Fearful of approaching you.
You've made your point very clear.

Thanks, for your contribution to my anxiety.

Spotted Blue Crow Part 2 (Am I Crazy?)

Reflection:

Consider your innermost thoughts.

Question:

Are you crazy?

Spotted Blue Crow Part 2 (Am I Crazy)? (scripture)

For the sake of Christ, then, I am content with weaknesses, insults, hardships, persecutions, and calamities. For when I am weak, then I am strong.

(2 Corinthians 12:10)

Two Red Chairs

There's nothing like a "soul-tie." Oh yes, my soul, which was broken, was connected to another soul, which was broken. The two souls connected and began an unhealthy exchange. Now my actions are a reflection of the bond that is hard to break but is, nevertheless, unfulfilling, unsatisfying, and unwilling to let go. In between the good moments, there's much turmoil and unhappiness. To even hope for a better future is exhausting. I've learned that sometimes in order to get a connection, there must be a disconnect.

Two Red Chairs

"We" just don't fit me.
I'm with you, and you're with me,
But "we," just don't fit me.

I am an independent woman, always have been.
You can stay or go.
I will be just fine.

In fact, who is this "we" benefitting?

The company was good.
Times we had were pleasant,
Some, not so much.

We met.
You were amused by my presence.
My appearance amused you more.

We learned of each other in the interim;
The superficial was "real."
We grew.

We grew in "love."

No, we grew in "lust."

No, we grew more and more "superficial."

Our adoration for one another's fake personas grew so strong...
The bond is unbreakable.
We are committed to one another's foolishness.

But, this "we" doesn't feel right to me.

"I love you."

continued

You love whom?

The front is real.
What we thought was light is pure shade.
But I never felt this "we" thing.

This thing is becoming explosive.
I've allowed me to become we, and now we're here,
Trying to figure out "us."

I miss you when you're gone, but don't want to be bothered.
"I" have enough to deal with.
Factors of evidence demonstrate our need for togetherness.
But "we" is just not working for me.

I had no idea what you were dealing with. Likewise,
I was a diamond in the rough.
I thought I was tough, but enough!

This "we" ain't for me.

Ok. I'm done.

The masks come off.

Like bananas being peeled, our true personas are revealed.

The frustration grows as we break up to make up.

The force behind our artificial commitment is stronger than the reality of us;
The reality of us is that there is no us;
there is no us because "we" can't be;
We can't be because "I" am no longer interested;
"I" am no longer interested, because you want to build from a foundation that was built from artificial characters,
Like in a movie... Oh yeah, we played those parts.

Forced together, grown into lust,
never having known true love;

nonetheless, claiming to be in something that neither of us has ever experienced, because neither of us knows the true meaning, never having the luxury of experiencing it. But "we" is where you want to be. Not me.

Looking back at all "you" and "I" have gone through,

I now sit
In front of our home.

"We" side by side in our Two Red Chairs.

Two Red Chairs

Reflection:

Consider a present or a past relationship.

Question:

Are you in a relationship with this person, or committed to each other's soul, which like soul food, fills you in a moment, but doesn't last? Are you willing to wait for that person who will contribute to your mind, body, soul, and spirit?

Two Red Chairs (scripture)

He restores my soul. He leads me in paths of righteousness for His name's sake.

(Psalms 23:3)

"SHUT UP AND FILL UP"

Simply: God told me to.

"SHUT UP AND FILL UP"

BUT SHE HAS SO MUCH TO SAY.
FROM HER MIND?
FROM HER HEART?

SSHHH...

INTERNALLY SHE'S STRUGGLING.
SHE'S SCREAMING TO BE HEARD.
LET ME OFFER YOU A PIECE OF WHAT I HAVE.

BUT SHE'S JUST A PIECE.

SHE'S MIXED WITH TOXINS.
PARTICLES SPILL OVER INTO HER PURITY. A MIXTURE IS MADE.
HER PURITY BECOMES POISONOUS.
DO NOT OPEN YOUR MOUTH.

BUT YOU SHOULD HEAR WHAT SHE'S THINKING.
PURE IS HER THINKING, "BUT OUT OF THE HEART, THE MOUTH SPEAKS."

HER HEART IS STONE.
AND STONES DO NOT SPEAK.
SILENCE.
MANY FORMS THEY DO COME.

BUT SHE'S NOT FULLY FORMED.

AGH. SHE HAS THE ANSWERS THAT YOU SEEK.
THEY'RE WRAPPED IN A PRETTY LITTLE BOW
IN HER MIND.
PLUS, SHE'S FINE AS WINE.
AGEING... GRACEFULLY,
SITTING, WAITING.

continued

DRINK, DRINK, DRINK.
NO.
SHE HAS NOT FULLY MATURED.

BUT SHE'S READY TO EXPLODE.
POP THE CORK!

NO.
KEEP A LID ON IT.

LET WHAT'S IN THE BOTTLE FLOW OUT.

SHE'S STRUGGLING AND NEEDS TO POUR OUT.
ADDICTION.

"OUT OF THE HEART THE MOUTH SPEAKS."
HER HEART IS STONE.

IT IS "I" WHO COMMANDED THE ROCK TO BE HIT FOR THE WATER TO RUSH FROM IT.

IT IS "I" WHO SAYS "SHUT UP AND FILL UP."

AND OUT OF YOU WILL FLOW RIVERS OF LIVING WATER.

"SHUT UP AND FILL UP"

Reflection:

Consider who you are and who you could be, what you are and what you will be, if you just shut up, and fill up. There will be seasons in your life where there will be certain positions you have to take. And in these seasons, no one is going to be checking for you. Pride will tell you to speak up, make yourself seen.

Question:

Will you recognize these seasons? Or will you continue to fail miserably in a position that is not yours to fill?

"SHUT UP AND FILL UP"
(scripture)

Three times I pleaded with the Lord about this, that it should leave me. But He said to me, My grace is sufficient for you, for My power is made perfect in weakness. Therefore I will boast all the more gladly of my weaknesses, so that the power of Christ may rest upon me.

(2 Corinthians 12:8-9)

My First Love

There is nothing like never knowing true love. Even worse, there is nothing like going through life never knowing what true love is, and thus settling or becoming comfortable with a counterfeit. Countless times I've told someone I loved them, or expressed my love for something without a genuine understanding of the term. I have remained in situations longer than I should have because of "love." It sounds so good and so fulfilling. Nevertheless, saying I love you was speaking such empty words with empty and contradictory actions that followed. "God is Love." The description of Christ's character is one which I have yet to find a comparison, even within myself.

My First Love

I Love you.

I Love you, too.

These shoes I love; this dress I love…

We are meant to be together. These shoes, this dress, are meant for me.
They go together and fit so perfectly.
You, I, and this outfit are a reflection of pure strategy.

But me? Oh I love me some me. Except for…
Those scars I bear from childhood, which I try to cover and act is if they don't exist;
Oh, and the cellulite that increases as my age… increases.

She went from being the youngest in the bunch to the oldest, from the boldest to the coldest, the kindest to the meanest.

Don't forget about her toes that she dares not to expose, because she chose… to continue to wear those shoes that she outgrew as a child, because she *loved* them.

She has a lot to undo, but undo she can't do. But when she meets her first love,
Everything will become new.

Physically and figuratively, she has a good side and bad.
The effort she puts in to keep from showing that which was not pleasing.
Exhausting.

Covering what she does not want to be revealed. But for her first love she will bare all.

See, He met me where I was and accepted me. Impeccable was His timing.
I was tired of love that didn't last,

Love I could not see, I could not feel; love that seemed as if it never existed,
Including the love I had for me.

Love with conditions was the only love I knew; Love that was inconsistent,
Partial,

Just like my love for you. Sometimes I feel it; sometimes I don't.

Those shoes—I only loved when they went with the right outfit. Just so happens, they only went with that one dress.

I have finally found a Love that is everlasting.

My First Love

Reflection:

Consider those whom you love. Consider your personal meaning of love.

Question:

What does love mean to you? Do you know what love is?

Refer to: 1 Corinthians 13: 4-8.

My First Love
(scripture)

Love must be sincere. Hate what is evil; cling to what is good.

(Romans 12:9)

And so I did.

Bio

Ves'Shawna Jackson was born and raised in Syracuse, New York. A single mother of four children, she strives to overcome any and all challenges, in Christ, while learning, evolving, and teaching others. She continues to gain wisdom, while deepening her walk with Christ. She aims to be delivered from anything that was not given to her by God, so that she can deliver all that He has placed in her. Shawna's walk with the Lord began in 2010, and she has not looked back.

In this book, I share with you my journey through creative writing (poems). You will learn of my personal place of surface level; how all seemed well when I was blind, but could see--with no vision. I was safe, with no refuge, and guarded with no protection. I had a story that I would "never" tell. But never say never. Here is my story.

> *Therefore do not be ashamed of the testimony about our Lord, nor of me his prisoner, but share in suffering for the gospel by the power of God, who saved us and called us to a holy calling, not because of our works but because of His own purpose and grace, which He gave us in Christ Jesus before the ages began* (2 Timothy 1:8-9).

CPSIA information can be obtained
at www.ICGtesting.com
Printed in the USA
BVHW030506300720
584608BV00001B/30